World of Music

Australia, Hawaii, and the Pacific

Deborah Underwood

Heinemann
LIBRARY

Chicago, Illinois

Designed by Victoria Bevan and Philippa Baile
Originated by Chroma Graphics (Overseas) Pte Ltd
Printed and bound in the United States of America,
North Mankato, MN.

12 11 10
10 9 8 7 6 5 4 3 2

**Library of Congress Cataloging-in-Publication
Data**
Underwood, Deborah.
World of music: Australia, Hawaii, and the Pacific /
Deborah Underwood.
p. cm.
Includes bibliographical references (p.   ) and index.
ISBN 978-1-4034-9894-6 (library binding -
hardcover)
1. Music--Australia--History and criticism--Juvenile
literature. 2. Music--Hawaii--History and criticism--
Juvenile literature. 3. Music--Oceania--History and
criticism--Juvenile literature. I. Title. II. Title: Australia,
Hawaii, and the Pacific.

ML360.U53 2007
780.99--dc22
2006100576

082010
005870RP

Acknowledgments

The author and publisher are grateful to the following
for permission to reproduce copyright material: Alamy
Images pp. 10 (Doug Steley), 19 (David Hancock),
20 (Edwin Remsberg), 25 (Photo Resource Hawaii),
31 (Greg Vaughn), 34 (Dennis Cox); Corbis pp. 4
(Albrecht G. Schaefer), 8 (Historical Picture Archive),
12 (Reuters), 13 (Eye Ubiquitous; Matthew McKee),
16–17 (Douglas Peebles), 18 (Paul A. Souders),
23 (Wolfgang Kaehler), 28 (Anders Ryman), 32
(Michael S. Yamashita), 33 (Historical Picture
Archive), 37 (John and Lisa Merrill), 38 (Bettmann);
Getty Images pp. 7 (Photographer's Choice), 15
(Stone), 42 (Sandra Mu); John Warburton-Lee
p. 21 (David Fanshawe); National Geographic/
Klaus Nigge p. 11; Redferns pp. 9 (Bob King), 35
(JM Enternational), 36 (Mick Hutson), 40 (Peter
Still), 43 (Andrew Lepley); Reuters p. 24 (Lucy
Pemoni); Sharlene Oshiro p. 41; Still Pictures
pp. 22 (Fotoarchiv), 26 (Patricia Jordan).

Cover photograph of Aboriginal Australian playing a
didjeridu reproduced with permission of Superstock/
Steve Vidler.

Illustrations by Jeff Edwards and Darren Lingard.

The publishers would like to thank Patrick Allen for
his assistance in the preparation of this book.

Every effort has been made to contact copyright
holders of any material reproduced in this book. Any
omissions will be rectified in subsequent printings if
notice is given to the publishers.

Disclaimer

All the Internet addresses (URLs) given in this book
were valid at the time of going to press. However,
due to the dynamic nature of the Internet, some
addresses may have changed, or sites may have
changed or ceased to exist since publication. While
the author and publishers regret any inconvenience
this may cause readers, no responsibility for any such
changes can be accepted by either the author or
the publishers.

Contents

Some words will be printed in bold, **like this.** You can find out what they mean by looking in the glossary.

Welcome to the Pacific

Fingertips tap out a **rhythm** on a sharkskin drum. The soft whistle of a wooden flute drifts across a sandy beach. A choir song spills from the door of a village church. The final chord of a **symphony** rings out in a concert hall. An electric guitar solo thrills a rock concert crowd. If you travel to **Oceania**, you might hear all these different kinds of music.

Oceania stretches over a huge part of the Pacific Ocean. It includes Australia, New Zealand, and around 25,000 Pacific islands. People live on about 1,500 of these islands. The Pacific Islands are often divided into three groups. Melanesia reaches to the north and east of Australia. The Fiji Islands, the Solomon Islands, and Papua New Guinea are part of Melanesia.

Micronesia lies to the north of Melanesia. Micronesia includes a group of 607 islands called the Federated States of Micronesia. It also includes many other islands, like the Marshall Islands, Guam, the Northern Mariana Islands, and Palau.

Polynesia covers a triangle-shaped area of ocean east of Melanesia and Micronesia. The corners are marked by New Zealand, Rapa Nui, and Hawaii. Polynesia's islands include Samoa, Tonga, and the Cook Islands.

This girl from Papua New Guinea is getting ready to perform with a village dance group.

Many lifestyles

Palm trees sway beside warm, sandy beaches in many parts of the Pacific. But Oceania also includes the scorching deserts of central Australia, New Zealand's steep snow-capped mountains, and Papua New Guinea's humid rain forests.

Before Europeans arrived in the Pacific around the 1500s, the people mostly lived in small groups. Today some still do. Only about 45 people live on tiny Pitcairn Island. But Oceania is also home to large, busy cities like Sydney, Australia, with its four million people.

Hundreds of different cultural groups can be found in the Pacific. In Papua New Guinea alone, around 700 different languages are spoken! Groups developed their own music, art, and religions. Because there are so many cultures there, Oceania is home to a wide variety of traditional music.

This map shows the vast area which Oceania covers. It includes Australia, New Zealand, Hawaii, and about 25,000 Pacific Islands. The music of Oceania is very varied—you might hear someone playing the **didjeridu** in Australia, hear a haka chant in New Zealand, or a hula song in Hawaii.

History of the Pacific Islands

Imagine you are moving to a deserted island with your family and friends. You'll travel by sea, in two long canoes joined side by side with poles. A sail made from woven leaves will catch the wind. You'll be at sea for weeks, but you won't have a cell phone, or even a compass! Instead, you will find your way by observing the Sun, the stars, wave patterns, and birds.

You must carry with you everything you'll need to survive on your new island. The plants and animals you bring will provide food. You'll also bring along something else: the music of your old home.

Slow spread of people

Many scientists believe humans arrived in Oceania at least 40,000 years ago. They came from southeast Asia and settled in Australia and on New Guinea.

People traveled by sea to other parts of Melanesia. From there humans spread to Micronesia. Polynesia was probably settled around 3,000 years ago. People traveled from Polynesia to New Zealand sometime over 1,000 years ago.

As people sailed to new places, they brought music from their homelands. Where islands were clustered together, people could trade with each other and share their music.

Waves of song

Sometimes songs capture the waves of the sea. On Micronesia's Yap Islands, song **melodies** often start on low notes. The notes get higher and higher, reach a peak, then get lower and lower. Songs repeat this pattern over and over. The up-and-down motion is like the falling and rising of ocean waves.

The sea's importance

Many of Oceania's people rely on the sea for food and transportation. Even today many islands can be reached only by boat.

Music made life at sea easier. Rowing songs helped people in canoes paddle in rhythm. In the Society Islands, if two canoes went out to sail, they sometimes brought drums along. The drum sounds helped the boats find each other in the ocean.

The sea is an important feature of life in many parts of Oceania.

Europeans arrive

In the 1500s, Europeans began to visit Oceania. As they settled in the region, they brought big changes.

Culture clash

Some Western traders came to the Pacific looking for sandalwood, a fragrant (strong-smelling) wood not found in Europe. Others turned land into farms to grow coconut and sugar. As more of their citizens moved to the area, Western governments moved in to protect their people and the land they'd taken. In the last half of the 1800s, nearly all of Oceania was controlled by European nations or the United States.

Traditional ways of life changed. Europeans moved some native people off their homelands. Many others died of diseases the Westerners brought. **Missionaries** who came to the Pacific wanted to stamp out local religions. Since music was part of these religions, they often banned traditional songs and dances. Some kinds of music survived and are still performed today. But other types were lost forever.

Trumpet danger

In 1642, the Dutch explorer Abel Tasman sighted New Zealand. When canoes approached his ship, his sailors heard a trumpet-like sound. They responded by playing a trumpet of their own. The next day, Tasman's ship was attacked, and four people were killed. The native people may have believed the trumpet call meant that Tasman's crew was planning to attack them.

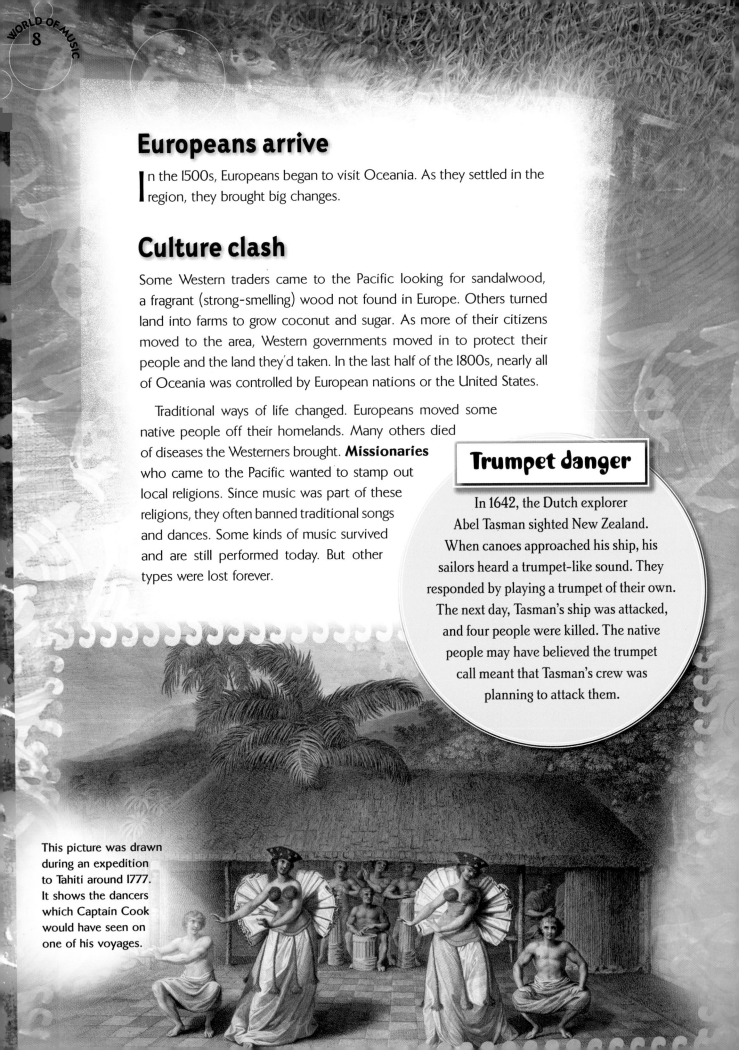

This picture was drawn during an expedition to Tahiti around 1777. It shows the dancers which Captain Cook would have seen on one of his voyages.

New sounds

Westerners brought new instruments and new styles of music. In the Pacific Islands, Western music often merged with traditional music to form new sounds.

In the past, traditional music and Western music did not mix much in New Zealand and Australia. However, symphony **orchestras** now sometimes feature guest artists playing ancient instruments. Rock bands also mix old and new sounds.

Mandawuy Yunupingu is the lead singer of Yothu Yindi. In 1992, he was named "Australian of the Year" for creating better relationships between Aboriginal and non-Aboriginal Australians.

Yothu Yindi

The Australian rock group Yothu Yindi combines traditional Australian instruments like **didjeridus** with drums and electric guitars. They even mix languages. Some songs are sung partly in a native Australian language and partly in English.

Traditional Music

What is the most important instrument in many Pacific cultures? It's something you don't need to build, blow, thump, or strum, and it's easy to carry around. It is the human voice! The words, not the tunes, are the most important parts of songs. In fact, many songs are chanted mostly at one **pitch**.

Some songs recorded a tribe's history. This was especially important because most places did not have written languages. Certain songs called on the power of spirit **ancestors**. Songs were sung to cast love spells or heal illnesses. In north Australia, there was even a special song to sing to stop it from raining!

Tattoo songs

Many Samoan men get tattooed from waist to knees. A tattoo artist dips a small comb into ink, then makes designs by using a mallet to tap the comb into the skin. Getting a tattoo takes days, and it is very painful. In the past, special tattoo songs were sung to distract the men during the process.

Singing can be heard throughout Oceania. These native people are singing in Goroka, Papua New Guinea.

Music and dance

In much of **Oceania**, music and dance are closely connected. Sometimes a kind of song and a kind of dance even share the same name. One doesn't make sense without the other, and neither would be performed alone.

Sound signals

In times before telephones and radios, musical instruments helped people communicate. If you were a young person in Polynesia, you might run to the beach if you heard a **conch** shell horn. The horn announced that a fishing boat was returning, maybe bringing your dinner! New Zealand natives listened for the sound of the village watchman beating on a slab of wood. This told them danger was approaching.

These children from Papua New Guinea are performing a seated dance.

Tuini Ngawai

New Zealand Maori, Tuini Ngawai (1910–1965) was a teacher and sheep-shearer who wrote more than 200 songs. She often set the words to familiar pop tunes.

Chants and songs

It is game time at a rugby stadium. As the crowd cheers, players from New Zealand's team, the All Blacks, face their opponents and begin shouting a fierce chant. As they shout, they crouch with their legs spread wide and slap their thighs and elbows. They glare, grunt, and sometimes even stick their tongues out. It is not surprising that their opponents look a bit nervous!

The players' chant is called a haka. In the past, haka were performed by warriors preparing for battle, but also just for entertainment. Today many New Zealand teams do a haka before a game. Haka refers to both the chant and the dance.

The **Maori**, New Zealand's native people, sing lots of different traditional songs. Most are sung in **unison**. Some songs have tunes. **Recited** songs like haka have **rhythms** but no **melodies**.

The All Blacks rugby team from New Zealand performs a haka before each game.

Magical music

In the past, Maoris chanted *karakia*, which were like magic spells. Some *karakia* were sung to heal broken bones or to slow down enemies. Others were meant to make weapons more powerful or to ward off bad luck. Today a *karakia* usually refers to a prayer or blessing.

Don't breathe!

Karakia had to be performed perfectly. If a singer made a mistake, the Maori believed the gods might punish, or even kill, the person. The sound needed to be unbroken, so singers could not breathe during the song. One person could sing a short *karakia* alone. Two people took turns singing longer *karakia*.

Maori children sang many kinds of songs, including breath-holding songs. They would compete to see who could sing longest on one breath. This was good training for singing *karakia* as adults.

Maori women sing *poi* songs as they twirl *poi*, pairs of balls connected with strings.

Australia's Dreaming songs

The native people of Australia are called **Aboriginal people**. Their stories tell that once Earth was flat and featureless. Then, creator spirits rose out of the ground. They included the Kangaroo, the Snake, the Crocodile, Rain, and many others. The time when the spirits roamed Earth was known as the **Dreaming**.

The spirits moved across the land and made mountains, rivers, animals, and plants. As they worked, they sang. The spirits also created people. The Kangaroo ancestor made kangaroos. He also made the group known as the Kangaroo people. The spirit, the land where he lived, the Kangaroo people, and kangaroos are all closely tied together. Aboriginal people still feel connected to the spirit ancestor and animal of their particular group.

Each spirit left songs for its people to use. These songs could be sung to do things like heal the sick, drive enemies away, or change the weather.

This map shows the position of Uluru, Australia's enormous sandstone rock. It sits right in the center of the country.

Aboriginal people believe many
Dreamtime ancestors lived on,
or traveled to, Uluru, shown here
(also see the map on page 14).

Calling up ancient power

An invisible **songline** traces the path where each spirit traveled. Some stretch across all of Australia. A songline does not only mean this invisible line. It also refers to the group of songs telling about the life of that creator spirit. Anyone who knows the songs can sing them anytime. They are often sung when people gather for ceremonies.

While they sing songs, people paint the bodies of the dancers. They use paints made from minerals ground up on a rock, then mixed with water.

In some areas, a stick with a chewed end serves as a paintbrush. Each group of Aboriginal people has its own designs. They may draw patterns on the ground with sticks. The people may clap hands or sticks together or play instruments as they sing.

These Dreaming songs are among the most powerful songs Aboriginal people sing today. When the songs are performed the right way, Aboriginal people believe they can tap into the power that each creator spirit left in the land.

Hula songs from Hawaii

As a crowd cheers, male dancers take the stage at a Hawaiian dance competition. They wear no clothes except the pieces of cloth that hang from their waists. Green leaves decorate their heads, necks, wrists, and ankles.

One man sings out a chant. Drums begin to thump. The dancers move as if they are rowing canoes, shouting out Hawaiian phrases in between lines of the song. The music speeds up. The men's bare feet stomp on the stage as they slap their thighs, strike poses with their arms, and turn their bodies from side to side.

These men are performing a Hawaiian hula. This particular hula tells the story of a great Hawaiian sailor. The actions of the hula dancers interpret the words of the song. Hula refers to both the song and the dance.

As elsewhere in Oceania, Hawaii's most important music is **vocal**. Hawaiian songs are called *mele*, which means both "poetry" and "music." *Mele* often contain hidden meanings. A song about a flower might really be talking about a person. The hula is one kind of *mele*. *Oli*, another type, are usually sung by one person without instruments.

Konggap songs

How do you catch a friend's attention? If you were one of the Yupno people in Papua New Guinea, you would sing your friend's personal song! Every Yupno has his or her own short tune, called a *konggap*. A mother chooses a *konggap* for her child shortly after birth, but the child can change it later.

Other Oceanian songs

Throughout Melanesia, Micronesia, and Polynesia, there are a huge number of traditional song types. Like New Zealand's recited songs and Hawaii's *oli*, many are chanted using just a few notes. Others use more pitches. They may be sung in unison, or people may sing different notes and rhythms at the same time.

Some songs honor the dead. Some keep track of tribal history. Children sing songs as they play certain games. On Rapa Nui (an island in the South Pacific), there were even insulting songs called *ēi* that could result in wars between tribes!

Hula dancers' movements express the words of songs. This dancer is performing in Kauai, Hawaii.

Wind Instruments

Australia's **didjeridu** looks like a simple wooden tube. But when a skilled musician plays it, it can make a variety of fascinating sounds, from buzzing to animal barks.

Traditional didjeridu-makers create the instruments from hollowed-out **eucalyptus** wood. How do they turn a solid branch into a wooden pipe? They don't. They search for branches that have had their insides eaten by insects! Today people make them out of other things, too, such as the plastic piping you'd find at a hardware store.

To play a didjeridu, buzz your lips into the end. Moving your tongue and cheeks makes the sound and **rhythm** change. You can even speak words or sing into the didjeridu as you play.

Circular breathing

Didjeridu players have to breathe, but when they take a breath, the instrument's sound keeps on going. How do they do it? They use a technique called **circular breathing**. They hold air in their cheeks. They push the air out with their cheek muscles as they grab a breath through the nose. This means they can take breaths without stopping the sound. This technique isn't just used for didjeridus. Someone who plays the oboe (a modern instrument found in **symphony orchestras**) might do it, too.

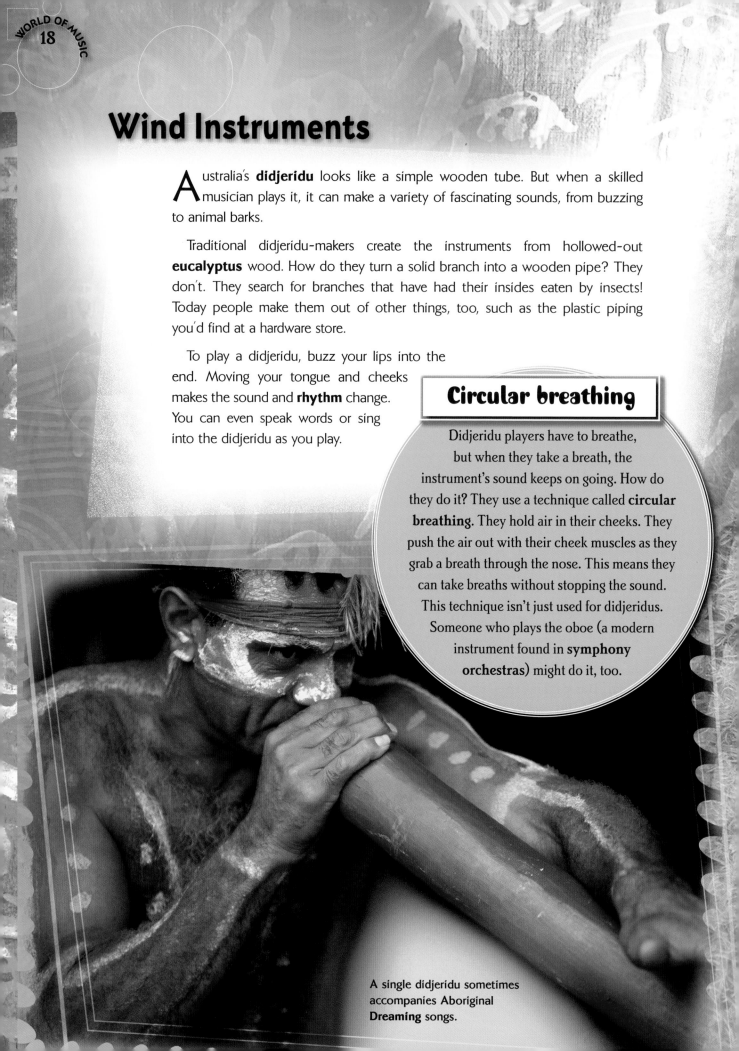

A single didjeridu sometimes accompanies Aboriginal **Dreaming** songs.

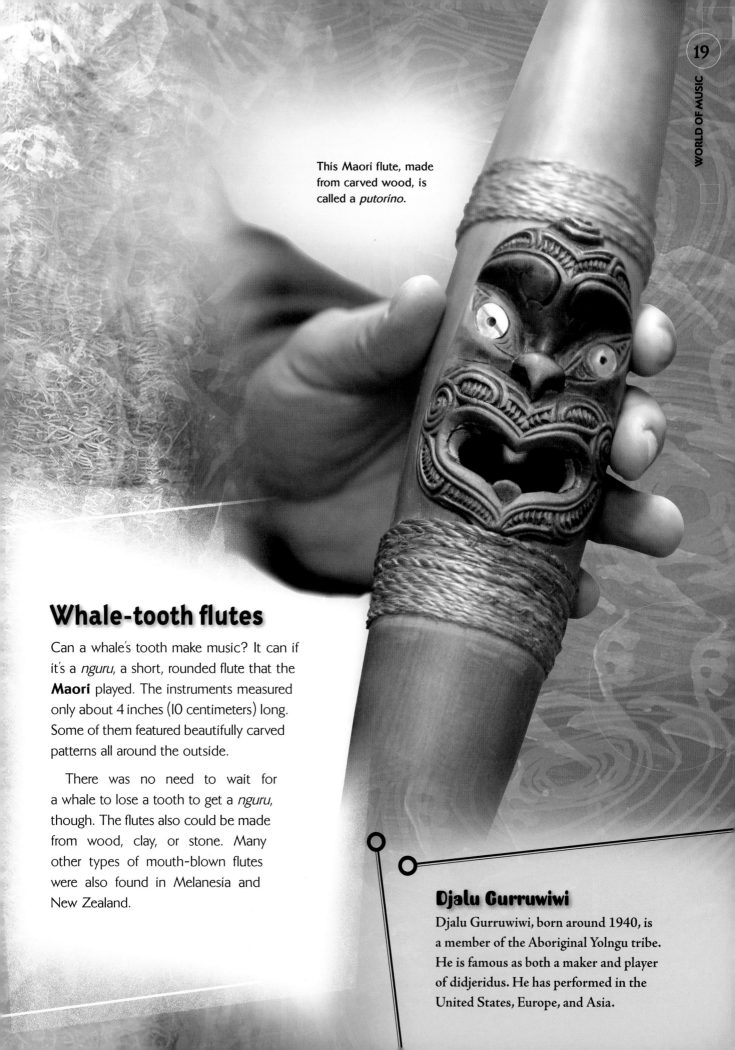

This Maori flute, made from carved wood, is called a *putorino*.

Whale-tooth flutes

Can a whale's tooth make music? It can if it's a *nguru*, a short, rounded flute that the **Maori** played. The instruments measured only about 4 inches (10 centimeters) long. Some of them featured beautifully carved patterns all around the outside.

There was no need to wait for a whale to lose a tooth to get a *nguru*, though. The flutes also could be made from wood, clay, or stone. Many other types of mouth-blown flutes were also found in Melanesia and New Zealand.

Djalu Gurruwiwi

Djalu Gurruwiwi, born around 1940, is a member of the Aboriginal Yolngu tribe. He is famous as both a maker and player of didjeridus. He has performed in the United States, Europe, and Asia.

Nose flutes

Tongan royalty did not have alarm clocks jolting them out of bed each morning. They were awakened by the gentle tones of **nose flutes**. Nose flutes are played not with the mouth, but with the nose. The player uses a finger or thumb to block one nostril and plays the flute with the other.

People played flutes with their noses because they believed that air from the nose was purer than air from the mouth. One reason the nose was believed to be more pure is that a mouth can tell lies, but a nose can't!

Nose flutes are found in Fiji, Papua New Guinea, and many parts of Polynesia. This one is from Guam, an island in the North Pacific Ocean.

Panpipes

Many people in the Solomon Islands play **panpipes**, lengths of bamboo gathered in a bundle or lined up in a row. The pipes are cut to different lengths, so each pipe plays a different **pitch**. By blowing into more than one pipe at once, a player makes **harmonies**.

In the past, someone out picking nuts could play his panpipes to call others to help carry the nuts home. Panpipes could also be used for more romantic reasons. A man might hide in the forest and play a tune. On hearing him, his girlfriend would sneak away to meet him.

Conch shell horns

Conch shell horns can be found throughout the Pacific. People make them from the shell of the conch, a large sea snail. To play a conch, you blow into a hole that is made by cutting off the end of the shell. A conch horn sounds like a trumpet, but a trumpet that plays only one note!

Conch horns were mostly used for signaling. In Hawaii, conchs were blown at the funeral of a chief or the birth of a chief's child. They also summoned warriors for battle.

Conch shell horns such as this one can be heard 2 miles (3.2 kilometers) away.

Rhythm Instruments

Y ou don't need to buy an instrument to make music. If you can clap or stomp, you already own a popular **rhythm** instrument. Clapping, snapping, and slapping parts of the body to make sounds is called **body percussion**.

You can make a lot of different sounds with body percussion. Samoans even have different names for different claps. Try clapping your hands together with flat palms. That's called a *pati*. Now, cup your hands and clap. Can you hear how the sound is lower in **pitch**? That kind of clap is called a *po*.

Samoan men do a dance called a *fa'ataupati*. The only accompaniment is the sound of the men clapping and slapping parts of their bodies. The dance doesn't last long, and the dancers end up with red skin where they slapped themselves!

Clapsticks

Two wooden sticks clapped together make a simple **percussion** instrument. **Clapsticks** often accompany Aboriginal songs. If you throw a flute away from you, it won't come back, but a clapstick might—some **Aboriginal people** use boomerangs as clapsticks!

Boomerangs can also be used as clapsticks, as this Aboriginal man shows. The man in the background of the picture is playing a **didjeridu**.

This native man, from Ambrym Island in the South Pacific Ocean, is communicating information using a slit drum signal.

Slit drums

A drum rhythm sounds through Papua New Guinea's warm, humid air. What is the drum telling you?

Many different sounds can be made by **slit drums**, which are found in Melanesia and parts of Polynesia. Some measure over 13 feet (4 meters) long! People make slit drums by carving a long slit in a log, then hollowing out the inside. Players make different sounds by hitting them with the sides or the ends of sticks.

An expert who studied one village's music in the 1930s learned what different drumbeats meant. One pattern announced an important person was coming. Another warned that the owner of the house where the drums were kept was angry. Slit drums were even used to report menus: one pattern meant that a special dessert was ready! Slit drums may still be used to gather people together or to announce a death.

Hula instruments

In Hawaii's modern hula, dancers use gently swaying hips and fluid arm motions to tell their stories. But ancient hula, or *hula kahiko*, uses sharper and more vigorous movement. *Hula kahiko* wouldn't be nearly as exciting without the thumping, rattling, and pounding of the traditional instruments that accompany it.

Drums

According to legend, a chief's son from Tahiti brought the *pahu* drum to Hawaii hundreds of years ago. Temple priests played the *pahu* to catch the attention of the gods. It once accompanied only certain important songs.

Today the *pahu* is played for a much broader range of music. Players use their fingers and palms to strike the **membrane**, the skin stretched over the top of the carved wooden frame. The vibration of the membrane makes the drum sound.

Some hulas are performed seated. The dancers chant and use arm movements to interpret the hula's words. Sometimes each dancer plays a small drum called a *puniu*, made from a fish skin stretched over half a coconut shell.

Traditional instruments accompany a hula. These dancers are also playing knee drums.

Ipu

During a *hula kahiko* performance, you'll probably see someone sitting on the ground playing an *ipu*, an instrument made from a large hollow **gourd**. Players make sounds by slapping the side of the gourd with their fingers, and by picking the gourd up and thumping it on the ground. Sometimes two gourds are joined together, one upside down on top of the other. This makes an instrument called an *ipu heke*. Often the hula teacher plays the *ipu* and chants while the students dance.

'Uli'uli

Brown feathers flutter in a hula dancer's hand. They decorate a rattle called an *'uli'uli*. Like the *ipu*, an *'uli'uli* is made from a gourd, but a much smaller one. The gourds are hollowed out and filled with seeds or pebbles.

This Hawaiian girl plays an *ipu heke*. It is often played while sitting down, but if played while standing, the bottom of the gourd is hit with the heel of the hand.

Skin drums

In Polynesia and Melanesia, drum membranes are often made from sharkskin. In Melanesia, these are also made from lizard skin.

Pacific Sounds

If someone flips on a radio station, you can tell in an instant whether you're listening to an **orchestra** or a rock band. But do you know why? What makes certain music sound the way it does?

Voices and instruments together

Many things affect the way music sounds. Is the music made by voices, instruments, or both? How are they mixed together? A lot of traditional Pacific music is performed either by one solo voice or by voices in **unison**. Drums or other **rhythm** instruments may play along, but the voices are most important.

Modern styles of island music feature many voices singing different parts of a song together in **harmony**. Sometimes more than ten different people sing at the same time!

An instrument's material affects the sound of its music. If you hit a metal gong, the sound lasts for a long time. Most **Oceanian** instruments are made of wood because it is a common resource in the area. This means the instruments' sounds die away quickly.

Instruments made of wood, like these **panpipes** from the Solomon Islands, give music a certain sound.

Notes next to each other on a piano are a half step apart. Two notes separated by another note are a whole step apart.

whole step

half step

Music's building blocks

The notes that make up music give the music a certain sound, too. Music is made up of different **pitches** or tones. A half step is the smallest **interval**, or distance, between notes in most Western music.

But in some parts of Oceania, the half step is not the smallest interval. Some Aboriginal songs use intervals much smaller than a half step. This music may sound strange and out of tune to Westerners,

just as Western music must have sounded strange to the first **Aboriginal people** who heard it.

The **range** of a **melody** means the distance between the lowest and highest notes. A tune that includes very low and very high notes has a wide range. Much of Oceania's traditional music has a narrow range. Some chants, like the Hawaiian *oli*, are sung mostly on one note.

Religious Influences

How can religion change musical history? Once Westerners discovered the Pacific Islands, **missionaries** started to arrive. They wanted islanders to give up their own religions and become Christians.

Because traditional music and dancing were part of native religions, many missionaries banned native music and dance. In some places, people hid their music from the missionaries so it would survive.

These children are lining up to enter a church in Samoa. Missionaries brought Christianity to Samoa around 1830.

Missionary music

Missionaries thought singing **hymns** would help the native people accept Christian beliefs. Some translated the words into native languages so the people could understand them. Sometimes missionaries set Christian texts to familiar island tunes, just as today Christian words may be set to rock music.

Hymns led to the development of a new type of choral music called *hīmene*. It began in Tahiti and spread to other parts of the Pacific. Some *hīmene* have sacred texts; others do not. Today most hymns in Western churches have four voice parts. *Hīmene* may have as many as 13!

Singing schools

The natives of some islands learned hymns easily. But some had trouble. Many weren't used to singing in **harmony**, since their own music was mostly in **unison**. In Hawaii, a missionary started a singing school in 1820. More quickly followed. Six years later there were eighty singing schools on one island alone.

Shell bands

Most islands didn't have organs or pianos, so one missionary in New Guinea formed a **conch** shell band to accompany hymns.

Reverend James Moulton

Reverend James Moulton (1863–1917) served as a missionary in Tonga. He tried to teach music using sol-fa, a way of teaching music in which each note is represented by a certain sound, like "do" or "re" or "mi." Unfortunately, putting some of these syllables together meant bad things in the Tongan language! He invented a new system using numbers instead. Tongan churches still use this method today.

Music and Community

The whistles of flutes float through the air in the Maprik area of Papua New Guinea. A group of men and boys moves toward a special building. The flutes warn women and young children to stay away—they are not allowed to see this procession. The people believe the flute sounds represent the voices of spirits.

The men are heading to an **initiation** ceremony. During initiations, children become adult members of their tribes. Many groups in Papua New Guinea have initiations. In some cultures, only initiated men are allowed to play, or even see, certain instruments.

Death songs

Funerals require special music in many parts of **Oceania**. Some groups of **Aboriginal people** believe a dead person's soul must travel to its final resting place. They sing songs to help the soul find the way. Each song represents a spot along the route the soul must travel. The songs are almost like a road map so the soul won't get lost.

Dreaming of music...

On the island of Tanna, if you want **composers** to write you a song, you give them a special sort of kava. They drink it and go to sleep, believing the new song will come to them in their dreams.

Kava music

Pohnpei is an island that lies about halfway between Hawaii and the Philippines. In Pohnpei, a group gathers to prepare **kava**, a relaxing traditional drink. Men put a special kind of plant root on large slabs of basalt, a type of rock. They squat down and begin pounding the root with smaller stones. As they pound, metallic sounds ring out like the clinking of large wind chimes. The rock slabs are chosen especially to make this ringing sound.

The men pound in **rhythm**, faster and faster. Different rhythms mark different stages in the process. Finally, the kava is ready! After the root has been pounded, they add water and pass the beverage around. The people may sing together after drinking the kava.

On Pohnpei, men use a particular rhythm for each stage in the kava-pounding process.

Sharing music with others

Throughout history, people have shared music and dances. Sometimes traveling performers tour and put on shows. Singers and dancers also come together at festivals. There, they entertain audiences and share music with each other.

Traveling entertainers

A group called the Arioi once lived in the Society Islands. They traveled from island to island entertaining with songs, dances, and plays. The traveling groups could be huge—one explorer who visited in 1774 saw a group made up of 700 Arioi in at least 60 canoes!

Tere parties

Have you ever sold candy to raise money for your school? If you lived in the Cook Islands, you might go to a nearby village and put on a show instead. Traveling groups like these are called *tere*, or "travel," parties. Schools, churches, and teams organize *tere* parties to raise money. The money might help pay for a new church building, or send the school band to a competition.

Dancers from all over the Pacific region compete at the Merrie Monarch Festival, which is held each year in Hilo, Hawaii.

Festivals

Festivals and competitions let people share their music and dance with a larger audience.

Hawaii's Merrie Monarch Festival celebrates Hawaiian culture. The festival, held each spring, lasts one week. The highlight is its hula competition. Hula groups come from far and wide to compete. On one night, the dancers perform *hula kahiko*, or ancient-style hula. On the next they dance hula *'auana*, or modern-style hula.

All of Oceania joins together in the Festival of Pacific Arts. The festival is held every four years. Different nations take turns hosting the event. The festival has grown since it began in 1972. Now more than 2,000 people from 27 nations participate. There are no competitions during the festival. However, musicians, dancers, and other artists work hard so they can be proud of how they represent their country.

King David Kalakaua

King David Kalakaua (left) was born in 1836. He ruled Hawaii from 1874 until his death in 1891. Known as the Merrie Monarch, he was responsible for bringing back the hula, which **missionaries** had banned. He called hula the heartbeat of the Hawaiian people.

Western Music

If you go to an Australian **folk music** concert, you might hear the sad sounds of "A Convict's Lament." The words were written in Australia by Irishman Frank MacNamara and set to an Irish tune. What took MacNamara so far from his homeland?

In 1787 British prisons were overcrowded, so prisoners were sent to Australia, where there was more space. The punishment was harsh, considering that some had stolen only a few handkerchiefs or some cheese. In 1788, after a grueling eight-month voyage, a fleet of ships arrived in Australia. Those aboard, including over 700 convicts on 6 transport ships, became Australia's first Western settlers.

More convicts came in the following years. Most were English, Irish, and Scottish. Their music became a part of Australia's heritage. MacNamara arrived in 1832. Many of his poems talk about the poor conditions the prisoners endured in their new home.

Waltzing Matilda

In 1895 Australian Banjo Paterson decided to write words for a Scottish folk tune. The words tell of a hobo who steals a sheep, then drowns himself to avoid getting caught. Today "Waltzing Matilda" is considered Australia's unofficial **national anthem.**

The Sydney Opera House perches on the edge of Australia's Sydney Harbor. Many famous opera singers have performed there, including Dame Kiri Te Kanawa.

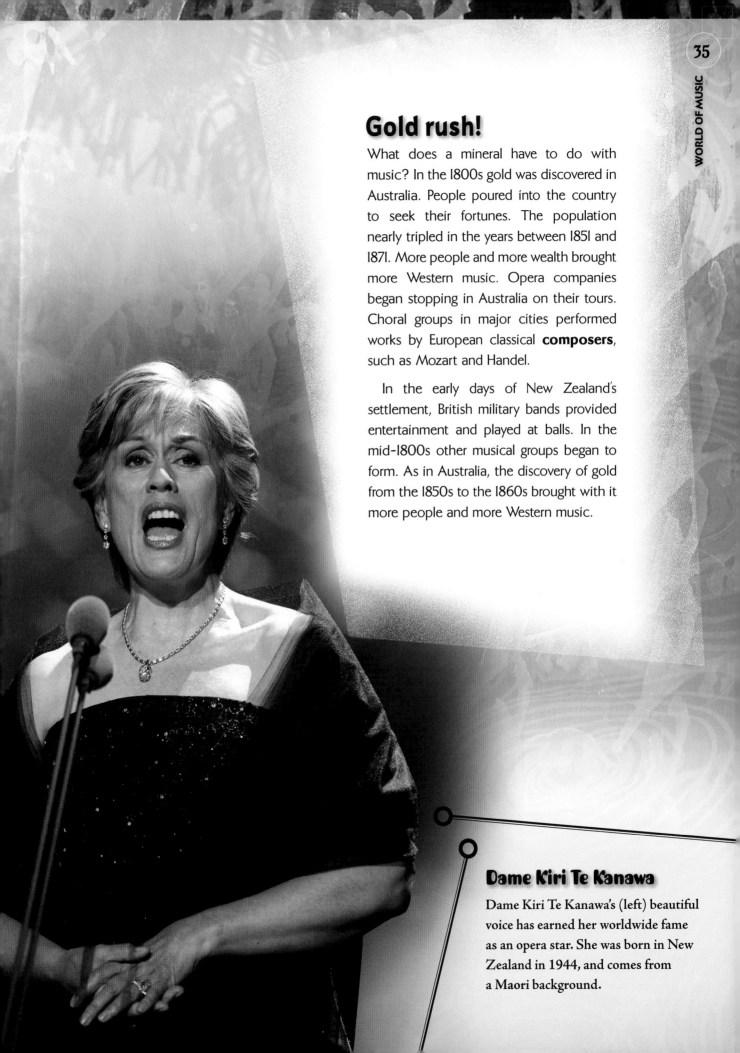

Gold rush!

What does a mineral have to do with music? In the 1800s gold was discovered in Australia. People poured into the country to seek their fortunes. The population nearly tripled in the years between 1851 and 1871. More people and more wealth brought more Western music. Opera companies began stopping in Australia on their tours. Choral groups in major cities performed works by European classical **composers**, such as Mozart and Handel.

In the early days of New Zealand's settlement, British military bands provided entertainment and played at balls. In the mid-1800s other musical groups began to form. As in Australia, the discovery of gold from the 1850s to the 1860s brought with it more people and more Western music.

Dame Kiri Te Kanawa

Dame Kiri Te Kanawa's (left) beautiful voice has earned her worldwide fame as an opera star. She was born in New Zealand in 1944, and comes from a Maori background.

The Strings of Hawaii

Just as **immigrants** brought their songs to Australia, foreigners brought Hawaii its two most important stringed instruments. The guitar was the first to arrive. It came as a result of some destructive cows!

Guitars come to the islands

In 1793 explorer George Vancouver gave Hawaii's King Kamehameha an interesting gift: some cattle. Over the years the herd grew and grew, trampling land and eating crops. In the 1830s King Kamehameha III, the son of King Kamehameha, brought Mexican cowboys to the islands to teach Hawaiians how to control the cattle. They brought a wealth of cattle-handling experience—and their guitars!

Hawaiians loosened, or slacked, the guitar strings so the strings made a chord that sounded nice even when there were no fingers on the **fretboard**. This style of guitar playing is called **slack key**.

The twang of the **slide guitar** also can be heard in Hawaiian music. Instead of pressing fingers on **frets**, the player slides something along the fretboard. The music slides from note to note, a bit like the way a siren slides from low to high **pitches**. These Hawaiian guitar styles influenced country-western and blues music in the mainland United States.

A slide on the fretboard gives
the slide guitar its unique sound.

In Hawaiian, *ukulele* means "jumping flea." It may have got this name because of the way a good player's fingers jump all over the instrument's fretboard.

The jumping flea

A Portuguese ship came to Hawaii in 1879. It carried hundreds of Portuguese immigrants—and a stringed instrument called a *machête*. Three of the Portuguese men began manufacturing and selling the instruments. Over time, makers changed the *machête* to make it easier to play. The **ukulele** was born!

The ukulele quickly became popular in Hawaii. At the 1915 World's Fair in San Francisco, visitors to the Hawaii building saw hula dancers and ukulele players. A ukulele craze swept the United States. Since songwriters didn't know the Hawaiian language, they made up words, resulting in silly songs like "Yaaka Hula Hickey Dula."

Music and Technology

If you sing your favorite song aloud, you can enjoy the sound, but only while you're singing. After you stop, the song vanishes. For most of **Oceania**'s history, music disappeared the moment it was performed. There was no way to record it.

However, starting at the end of the 19th century, recording equipment became available. The sound of a **symphony orchestra** or a tribal song could be captured and carried all over the world.

This U.S. soldier is playing an American-made piano in Guam. The picture was taken in 1944, a year before World War II ended.

Traveling tunes

Imagine living on a small Pacific island in the 1930s. A **missionary** comes to your village. He brings a mysterious wooden box with him. It holds a hand-cranked **phonograph**, a machine that plays music stored on flat, circular pieces of plastic called records. All of a sudden you can hear music you've never heard before.

Records helped Western music spread throughout Oceania. Ship crews and missionaries brought record players and records with them on their journeys. Ship workers also introduced instruments such as the guitar and **ukulele** to new areas.

During World War II (1939–1945), American and Japanese troops were stationed in the Pacific Islands. They brought their records, as well as instruments like harmonicas and guitars. U.S. military bases set up radio stations. Islanders listened to these broadcasts and heard music that was popular in the United States.

Saving and sharing songs

Recordings also help preserve traditional music. Older people can record songs for their children and grandchildren to hear. Special libraries collect recordings and save them for the future.

Small cassette tapes were invented in the 1960s. With battery-operated players, anyone could make recordings without needing power outlets or heavy equipment. People could travel to remote areas and collect a culture's songs.

Today, music lovers can download music and music videos from the Internet. (However, there are laws about downloading music and videos—please check with an adult before you do so.) This means that even a teenage rock band on a remote Pacific island can share its recordings with the world.

Alice Moyle

Alice Moyle (1908–2005), an Australian **ethnomusicologist**, traveled to many parts of Australia and recorded more than 400 tapes of **Aboriginal** music. She also worked to help educate people about Aboriginal culture.

Pacific Music Today

R ock, pop, jazz, classical, **folk**, and hip-hop music can all be found in **Oceania** today. Australia has produced popular modern musicians such as Kylie Minogue and Nick Cave. Australian bands AC/DC and INXS gained international fame. Tens of thousands of people gather for Australia's 10-day Tamworth Country Music Festival each January. In the 1990s, tribute bands—bands that dress up and play the songs of famous rock bands—became popular in Australia.

Around the same time, the New Zealand group Moana and the Moahunters introduced **Maori** pop music to an international audience, mixing Maori chants and instruments with dance **rhythms**.

Another New Zealand band, Te Vaka, brings together artists from Tuvalu, Tokelau, the Cook Islands, Samoa, and New Zealand. They play traditional **slit drums** along with modern instruments like the electric guitar. Most of their songs are sung in the language of Tokelau. *Te Vaka* means "the canoe"—a fitting name for a band that joins many islands together.

Australia's Kylie Minogue is an internationally known pop star. Kylie began her music career in 1987, and has gone on to have international success with songs such as "Can't Get You Out of My Head."

Hawaiian tourists and locals alike enjoy listening to Hawaiian music in island clubs. Eddie Kamae, a **ukulele** player, co-founded The Sons of Hawaii in 1960. The group played together for decades. The Makaha Sons also perform modern Hawaiian music. When Hawaiian musicians became fascinated by a type of music from Jamaica, they created **Jawaiian** music, which blends Hawaiian and **reggae** music.

The Makaha Sons from Hawaii are known for their rich **vocal harmonies.**

Return to native roots

Starting in the 1960s, many islands gained their independence from Western governments. Aboriginal Australians and Maori people fought to get back tribal lands that Europeans took from them many years before. As the rights of native people received more attention, interest in traditional cultures rose. This brought renewed interest in traditional songs, instruments, and dances.

Protest songs

Musicians often use popular songs to protest unfair treatment of native people. Sometimes song lyrics demand change. The song "Treaty" by Australian group Yothu Yindi speaks of a need for an agreement between **Aboriginal people** and the Australian government. Many songs by New Zealand hip-hop group Upper Hutt Posse speak of racism and of the problems brought by Westerners.

Joining ancient and modern

Today Oceania's music reflects its vibrant mix of cultures and traditions. Many Aboriginal Australians are fond of country music. Hundreds of brass bands can be found in Tonga. Island string bands combine guitars, ukuleles, banjos, and even violins.

Traditional music and ceremonies can be found in everyday life. At a Hawaiian wedding, someone may blow a **conch** shell horn to begin the ceremony. At a Maori meeting house, you may be welcomed with a ceremony called a *powhiri*. The hosts sing traditional songs, and you may be asked to respond with a song from your own country.

A Maori ceremony called a *powhiri* welcomes guests to a meeting house.

Lorenzo Lyons

The Reverend Lorenzo Lyons was born in 1807 and arrived in Hawaii in 1832. He remained in Hawaii until his death in 1886. Lyons wrote the words for one of Hawaii's most beloved songs, "Hawaii Aloha." After meetings or concerts, people often join hands and sing the song together.

In today's Oceania, you can hear everything from *karakia* to country western, *haka* to hip-hop, and brass bands to Beethoven **symphonies**. You might find a girl practicing the violin, an old man teaching a ukulele class, or an Aboriginal person giving **didjeridu** lessons. A village elder might play a drum to accompany a tribal ritual in Papua New Guinea, while a rock drummer in Sydney pounds out a solo before cheering fans in a stadium.

So, what does Pacific music sound like? There's no one answer! Instead, all the many types of music, from traditional to modern, combine to form a musical feast for visitors and local people alike to enjoy.

Jake Shimabukuro

Hawaiian musician Jake Shimabukuro (left) was born in 1976. He plays the ukulele—but don't expect him to play traditional Hawaiian songs. Instead, he plays jazz, blues, rock, bluegrass, and even classical pieces. He's famous for his lightning-fast fingers and for developing new playing techniques.

A World of Music

	String Instruments	Brass Instruments	Wind Instrument
Africa	*oud* (lute), *rebec* (fiddle), *kora* (harp-lute), *ngoni* (harp), musical bow, one-string fiddle	*kakaki* or *wazi* (metal trumpets), horns made from animal horns	*naga*, *nay sodina* (flutes), *arghul*, *gaita* (single-reed instruments), *mizmar* (double-reed instrument)
Australia, Hawaii, and the Pacific	**ukulele** (modern), guitar (modern)		flutes, **nose flutes**, **didjeridus**, **conch** shell horns
Eastern Asia	*erhu* (fiddle), *dan tranh, qin, koto, gayageum* (derived from *zithers*)	gongs, metallophones, xylophones	*shakuhachi* (flute), *khae* (mouth organ), *sralai* (reed instrument)
Europe	violin, viola, cello, double bass, mandolin, guitar, lute *zither*, hurdy gurdy (folk instruments)	trumpet, French horn, trombone, tuba	flute, recorder, oboe, clarinet, bassoon, bass clarinet, saxophone, accordion, bagpipes
Latin America and the Caribbean	*berimbau* (musical bow), *guitarrón* (bass guitar), *charango* (mandolin), *vilhuela* (high-pitched guitar)	trumpet, saxophone, trombone (salsa instruments)	*bandoneon* (button accordion)
Western Asia	*sitar, veena, oud, dombra, doutar, tar* (lutes), *rebab, kobyz* (fiddles), *sarod, santoor, sarangi*	trumpets	*bansuri, ney* (flutes), *pungi/been* (clarinets), *shehnai, sorna* (oboes)

Percussion Instruments	Vocal Styles	Dance Styles
balafon (wooden xylophone), *mbira* (thumb piano), bells, **slit drums**, friction drums, hourglass drums, conventional drums	open throat singing, Arabic style singing: this is more nasal (in the nose), and includes many trills and ornaments	spiritual dancing, mass dances, team/formation dances, small group and solo dances, modern social dances
slit drums, rattles, drums, **clapsticks**, **gourds**, rolled mats	*oli* (sung by one person), *mele* (poetry), hula, *himene* (choral music), **Dreaming** songs	hula, seated dances, *fa'ataupati* (clapping and singing), haka
taiko (drums)	*p'ansori* (single singer), *chooimsae* (verbal encouragement), folk songs	Peking/Beijing Opera, Korean **folk** dance
side drum, snare drum, tambourine, *timpani* (kettle drums), cymbals, castanets, bodhran, piano	solo ballad, work song, **hymn**, plainchant, opera, Music Hall, cabaret, choral, homophony (**harmony**, parts moving together), polyphony (independent **vocals** together)	jig, reel, sword dance, clog dance, *mazurka* (folk dances), flamenco, country dance, waltz, polka, ballet, *pavane, galliard* (1500s)
friction drum, steel drums, bongos (small drums), congas (large drums), *timbales* (shallow drums), maracas (shakers), *guiro* (scraper)	toasting	*zouk* (pop music), tango, lambada, samba, *bossa nova* (city music), rumba, mambo, *merengue* (salsa)
tabla drum, *dhol* drum,, tambourine, *bartal* cymbals, bells, sticks, gongs	bards, *bhangra* (Punjabi), *qawwali* (Sufi music), throat singing, *ghazals* (love poems)	*bhangra, dabke* (traditional dances), Indian classical, whirling dervishes, belly dancing

Glossary

Aboriginal people native people of Australia

ancestor relative who lived centuries ago

body percussion making sounds by clapping, snapping, or slapping parts of the body

circular breathing while playing an instrument, pushing stored air out with cheek muscles while at the same time breathing in through the nose so there is no break in the sound

clapsticks wooden sticks that are hit together

composer person who writes music

conch type of large shell or the sea creature that lives inside it

didjeridu Australian wind instrument usually made from a hollow log

Dreaming according to Aboriginal beliefs, the time when spirits created people, animals, and land features

ethnomusicologist someone who studies the music of a particular region

eucalyptus type of evergreen tree native to Australia

folk music music that is handed down in communities over many years. It is not usually written, but passed on by imitation and listening.

fret bar on a guitar that shows where the notes change

fretboard part of a guitar or ukulele where the fingers press against strings to make chords

gourd type of hard-shelled fruit

harmony combination of similar musical notes

hymn religious song

immigrant person who lives in a foreign country

initiation ceremony during which children become adult members of a tribe

interval distance between two notes

Jawaiian combination of Hawaiian music and Jamaican reggae

kava popular drink made from a pounded root

Maori native people of New Zealand

melody tune of a song

membrane skin stretched over the top of a drum

missionary person who brings a new religion to an area

national anthem official song of a country, usually sung at special events

nose flute flute played with air blown out through a nostril

Oceania Australia, New Zealand, and the island regions Melanesia, Micronesia, and Polynesia

orchestra large group of trained musicians playing a range of instruments

panpipes wind instrument made of bamboo pipes tied together

percussion instrument that produces sound when struck or shaken

phonograph instrument that plays recorded music by running a needle over flat, plastic discs

pitch musical tone

range distance between lowest and highest notes of a song

recite to repeat a song from memory before an audience

reggae type of Jamaican music

rhythm beat behind a piece of music

slack key style of guitar playing in which strings are loosened to change tuning

slide guitar style of guitar playing in which something is slid over the fretboard to change pitch

slit drum hollowed log with a slit cut in it

songline series of songs about a spirit ancestor, from Australia. Also, the physical path that the ancestor traveled across the land.

symphony long piece of music written for orchestra, usually in three or four sections

ukulele small, four-stringed Hawaiian instrument

unison when different voices or instruments sound the same notes at the same time

vocal produced by the voice

Further Information

Books

Bartlett, Anne. *The Aboriginal Peoples of Australia.* Minneapolis: Lerner, 2001.

Currie, Stephen. *Exploration and Discovery– Australia and the Pacific Islands.* Detroit, Mich.: Lucent, 2004.

Theunissen, Steve. *The Maori of New Zealand.* Minneapolis: Lerner, 2002.

Websites

National Library of New Zealand
http://discover.natlib.govt.nz

Indigenous Australian Culture
http://dreamtime.net.au/index.cfm

World Music Information
http://worldmusic.nationalgeographic.com

Recordings

Fanshawe, David. *Spirit of Melanesia* (Saydisc Records, 1998)

Fanshawe, David. *Spirit of Micronesia* (Saydisc Records, 1995)

Hudson, David. *The Art of the Didjeridu: Selected Pieces 1987–1997* (Black Sun Records, 1997)

Various. *Spirit of Polynesia* (Saydisc Records, 1995)

Organizations

Archive of Maori and Pacific Music
The University of Auckland
Private Bag 92019
Auckland, New Zealand
www.arts.auckland.ac.nz/research/index. cfm?P=435

Australian Institute of Aboriginal and Torres Strait Islander Studies
GPO Box 553
Canberra ACT 2601
Australia
www.aiatsis.gov.au

SOUNZ
Center for New Zealand Music
PO Box 10042
Wellington, New Zealand
www.sounz.org.nz

Index